THE BEE BOOK

THE BEE BOOK

by
JAKOB STREIT

Illustrations by
Jesùs Gabán

Translated from German by
Nina Kuettel

AWSNA

Printed with support from the Waldorf Curriculum Fund

Published by:
The Association of Waldorf Schools
of North America
Publications Office
65–2 Fern Hill Road
Ghent, NY 12075

Title: *The Bee Book*
Author: Jakob Streit
Editor: David Mitchell
Translator: Nina Kuetell
Copy Editor and Proofreader: Ann Erwin
Illustrations: Jesùs Gabán
© 2010 by AWSNA
ISBN # 978-1-936367-00-9

Printed by McNaughton & Gunn
Saline, MI 48176 USA
(May 2010)

TABLE OF CONTENTS

During the Winter Sleep

Deep snow is piled on the roof of the bee house. The cold winter wind howls and blows the white flakes through the branches of the silent, bare trees. Inside the farmhouse little Oliver presses his forehead against the windowpane and watches the swirling flakes. "See, Grandfather," he happily cries. "The snowflakes are like the bees, the way they also fly so crazily in the air in the summer!"

"It could be," comes the reply from next to the warm stove. "You could call the snowflakes the winter bees, but you won't be spreading their honey on your bread!" Grandfather laughs.

By the time Oliver understands the joke, the strongest wind gust yet lifts a white maelstrom from the bee house roof. "Woohoo, Grandfather! Look at that! It wants to tear off the roof of the summer bees' house. Then they would have to dance with the winter bees!"

From near the stove, another reply comes, with certainty. "The bee house will hold fast. I drove the nails into the wood myself with a heavy hammer. Those boards and beams will stay together."

"Grandfather, what are the bees doing now? Do they notice that a storm wind is blowing?"

"They are resting quietly, Oliver, and are cuddled up very close to one another. Every little bee holds tight to another. That is how they keep each other warm, and the queen is in the middle."

"When they wake up and can't visit any flowers, will they starve?"

"No, not at all," replies Grandfather. "They stored away honey all last summer in some of the honeycomb chambers. They take a few drops of it when they wake up hungry and then they go back to sleep."

"Don't they freeze when it's ice-cold outside and we don't heat the bee house?"

"You have to realize, dear Oliver, that there is a lot of sunshine hidden in the summer nectar drops. In winter it warms their bodies. Even the hive becomes warm from it. Of course, sometimes it happens that an old bee dies during the winter. The others carry her outside on a warmer day. She falls from the landing board onto the blanket of snow on the ground. If a bird flies by, it will pick up the dead bee because it can't find any little worms in the snow.

"But the bees don't like to trouble their sisters. So, often, when they feel they are going to die, they will loosen themselves from the warm colony. With effort they drag themselves to the exit and fly out with their last strength into the snow and bury themselves in a white grave."

"Grandfather, doesn't the fly hole have to be closed during the long, cold winter?"

"No, a tiny crack should remain open, just wide enough that a bee can slip through easily. If it is a strong colony, it must be open even a little further. Bee folk also breathe in winter. Fresh air comes into the house through this opening. You must never cover up the entrance or the whole hive could suffocate!"

"Grandfather, does such a hive ever die like people do?" asks Oliver.

"When the queen dies, Oliver, the bees cannot live much longer without her. If there is no new queen to take her place, yes, a great extinction comes upon the colony. One bee after the other will go down and the hive will become a house of the dead."

Grandfather continues, "Soon it will be Easter, Oliver. Then you may come with me to the bee house. I will open the back door of the box for every hive and tap on the window. Then you can listen carefully to what kind of sound the colony announces. If their wings make a whooshing sound like 'shshsh,' that is a good sign that the queen is still alive. But if she died during the hard winter, then, after a knock on the glass, the bees buzz a long, quiet, mournful tone, as if they were crying. Such a hive will live only a short time longer if it is left alone. But if one can give a new queen to a dying colony, then it is saved."

"Where do the new queens come from?" asks Oliver.

"I will tell you about that soon. You are old enough now to be a big help to me in the bee house. Would you like that?" asks Grandfather.

"I would really like that – if you tell the bees they should not sting me too much."

"We'll see about that," Grandfather laughs. "But right now, I have to go get some hay out of the loft." With these words, he leaves the living room. Oliver goes back to the window and looks down to the bee house that stands lonely in the snowfall and hides such mysterious wonders.

Suddenly he jumps to the stove, gets his clogs from under it, and slips them on. He pulls his cap over his ears, leaves the houses, and runs through the wind and snow down to the bee house. He wants to check to make sure that each of the little doors is open a small crack. Yes, it is exactly as Grandfather told him: He can stick in just the tip of his little finger. The wind blows cold and sharp through his clothing. Oliver quickly stomps back into the warm house, happy that Grandfather wants to tell him more about the bees and that he can help take care of them this year.

THE AWAKENING

By the end of February, the last of the snow has melted off the shingles of the bee house. In the fields, the hibernating ground is showing through the snow in big, yellow-brown patches. Finger-wide green tips of sprouting snowbells are peeking out, and the sun shines warm in the blue sky.

A mild breeze, full of sunny brilliance, wafts through the narrow flight entrance and into the beehive. The bees are barely stirring in the dark, quiet room. The sunny breeze plays around the feelers and wings of the little insect closest to the front, "Wake up! Wake up!" Ooh, it tickles! The little bee turns her head. She twitches a little bit and, half asleep, drags herself toward the exit.

When the little bee is on the landing board, she is fully awake, just as the Sun smiles at the sleepyhead, "What is the matter, little bee, that you do not even wave at me with your wings?"

"Oh, Sun Mother, just wait, we will wave at you. But first, my sisters and the queen must know that you are here again, and that the cold, white world is changing!" The little bee quickly disappears, buzzing happily, inside the dark gate. "Buzz, buzz, buzz…the Sun is here! Buzz, buzz, buzz…the sky is bright!" she quietly sings. Soon ten, twenty, a hundred wings begin to stir. A line of chipper, brisk bees scurries toward the exit. There is a tumbling throng at the narrow crack of the gate. Two bees cannot squeeze through it together. When the Sun sparkles around them on the landing board, their wings whir even stronger, and – swoosh! – the first ones lift into the air. They hover around the gate, up and down, singing.

During these days, Oliver goes often to the bee house. He is waiting impatiently for the first flight day. So, at this very moment he happens to be there and sees the glittering wings. His heart beats faster as he stretches his head closer to the landing board. He listens to the humming, sunny sounds, happy to see the bees in front of the gate tumbling over each other so cheerfully. He observes how some of them perch next to the wooden wall of the little house and deposit a brownish dab of something from their bodies. "Oh, look," he says to himself. "I will ask Grandfather if they are laying their first eggs here."

Suddenly Oliver notices that one bee is diligently gnawing at the wooden doorframe, probably trying to enlarge the exit. Oliver quickly runs up to the workshop where Grandfather is fixing a wagon wheel. "Come quick! Come quick, Grandfather!" he cries breathlessly, pulling on Grandfather's sleeve. "The bees can't get out of their house. They're gnawing at the little gate, and some of them have laid brown eggs by the wall. Hurry, come see!"

Grandfather smiles, "That must be Easter eggs, don't you think?

"Come on now, Grandfather. They will surely break their wings and legs if they butt up against the wood."

"Just let me finish hammering in this nail, and then I will be there."

When they are both standing by the edge of the bee house, Grandfather points to the brownish specks and says, "You see, if the bees had not been able to deposit these little specks from their bodies, they would become sick. It is the leftover honey that they sucked in during the winter. Now, they clean it out of themselves." Grandfather stands in front of the bee house and gently slides the opening apart with his hands. "I will open it only a little, for there will still be some cold days."

"Grandfather, is the queen also awake now? Will she come out on the board, into the sunshine?"

"No, Oliver, she does not come outside. She is awake and will begin laying the first eggs as soon as the hazelnut bushes over there let go of their golden pollen. That is like golden flour for the bees. They make very tiny loaves of bee bread out of it and feed it to the young ones to eat when they hatch from their eggs. They also get their first spring bread from the willow catkins. That is why we hope people will not break off big bunches of them to fill their flower vases. Then the young bees would have to go hungry."

Grandfather walks back up to the house, but Oliver stays at the bee house. Suddenly, he hears an irregular buzzing. He sees how one bee is dragging another and falls from the landing board with it to the ground. She flies up again, but the other stays on the ground. Oliver gently leans down to get a closer look. Since she is moving neither leg nor wing, but just lying there on her back, he realizes the little bee is dead. He carefully takes hold of one wing and lifts it onto his hand. How light it is, just like a feather! The stiff body is bowed, the little feet screwed up tight, and the unmoving wings are transparent. Oliver lays her back down on the ground. He quietly goes over to the hazelnut bush and shakes the budding branches. But they are still asleep and do not loosen their pollen dust yet. "I will try it every day now so that I will know when the queen is laying eggs," he thinks, and slowly returns to the workshop.

SUN BREAD

As the first little snowbell flowers are ringing in the spring breeze, during the warm night, the buds of the hazel bushes soften. In the morning, when Oliver tickles them, his finger comes away covered in yellow pollen dust. He touches it to his tongue and tastes the delicate flour. *Now the queen will start laying eggs*, he thinks. *But I will stay here to see if a bee comes to get some hazel flour.*

Oliver waits quietly by the bush. Before long he hears something buzzing past his ear, and – sure enough – a bee alights on one of the golden buds. Her legs swiftly dig out the gold dust and soon her body and wings are gilded gold. Suddenly she pauses and begins to brush herself with her legs. Oliver goes closer but holds his breath so he will not blow the bee away.

Now Oliver can clearly see how the bee sweeps all of the pollen on to her back legs until it looks like she is wearing leggings. The little bee flies to a few more buds, brushes and kneads again, until finally she is carrying a thick, golden layer.

All at once, she flies back toward the bee house. Oliver runs after her, but she slips inside before he can get there. So Oliver watches the flight of the other bees.

Among those returning to the hive, many bees are carrying just such little balls of gold. "Oh, I would like to taste such a bee loaf of bread. It must be good!" Oliver is amused to watch how the bees hurriedly come out of the dark entrance, even crawling over the backs of the bees returning.

Just then one bee shoots out very hastily and runs over a returning bee loaded down with pollen. Whoosh! One of the leggings is stripped away and rolls to the front of the landing board. Now wearing only one legging, the little bee disappears into the darkness.

I'm going to get the other bit of pollen that fell off, thinks Oliver. He moistens the tip of his index finger with his tongue and carefully pushes it toward the landing board. He dabs at the yellow pollen. It sticks to his wet skin. Then he slowly pulls back his hand and puts the sun bread in his mouth. Oh, it is delicious! It tastes sweet, but has a slightly sour aftertaste.

Oliver runs joyfully up to the house and blusters around in the kitchen where his mother is just pouring soup into the bowls. "Where have you been today?" she asks.

"Mother," he exclaims, "I don't need any soup today! I've already eaten. Do you know what?" Puzzled, she looks at the boy and does not know what he is talking about. "I ate sun bread!" he shouts joyfully and winks at Grandfather.

Grandfather asks, "Did you lick the hazel buds?"

"No, it was a real, round, sun bread. I took it off the front of the landing board. I happened to be watching when a bee lost it."

"I'll be jiggered," Grandfather says. "You are lucky. You don't see that every day."

At the table, the boy tells how the bees gathered the golden flour from the hazel buds and made little leggings with it and how funny it was when they tumbled over each other on the landing board. But after he asks for his third bowl of soup, his mother says, "I guess sun bread makes you hungry!"

Queen Inspection

It is now the week before Easter and Grandfather says to Oliver, "Come with me to the bee house. Today we will do the queen inspection. Then we will know if the queens have stayed alive through the winter."

Before Grandfather and Oliver step inside the bee house, they stop to watch for awhile how the bees are flying around. "Grandfather, look at the entrance to the back hive. Almost no bees are flying."

"I noticed that too," he says. "There's something not quite right there. It could be a hive in mourning. You see, when a queen dies, for the colony it is the same as if one day the Sun suddenly stopped shining for us people. If that were to happen, we would fumble around in the dark and die miserably."

The key to the bee house creaks in the lock. It has rusted during the winter. Oliver and Grandfather step inside. It is dark. Once the window shutters are opened, Oliver recognizes the many hive boxes, one row on the bottom and one on the top. They are all numbered. A small chalkboard hangs next to each one with notes written on it.

"Look here, Oliver, this is the first job you will do for me in the bee house. All these chalkboards must be wiped clean. Now begins a new bee year, and every hive gets its own calendar." With these words, Grandfather lifts off the lid of the first box, removes the straw pillows that protected the colony from the cold, and uncovers the inside window. "Pay attention, my boy, I will now knock on the glass pane with my finger. Listen carefully how the bees answer!" After the knocking, Oliver could hear an energetic 'shss' sound. "Did you hear?" Grandfather asks. "This colony is healthy and strong. We can put the lid back on."

The rustling good news is heard several more times. The sound is strong with the large colonies and a little weaker with the smaller ones. Oliver is allowed to knock as well. In front of the last window, he says, "Grandfather, you knock."

As soon as the noise sounds on the glass, a low whining sound answers, long and low, as if it would not stop. "Oh my," Grandfather says. "It is the mourning song. And this was once my best honey colony." He crouches thoughtfully in front of the hive box. Finally he turns to Oliver, sadly hanging his head, and commands, "Run up to your mother and get half a glass of thick sugar water."

While Oliver hurries away, Grandfather removes the sliding window from the box. He takes a long tool and sweeps the dead bees on to a shovel. When Oliver returns with the sugar water, Grandfather says, "Now we will put the rest of the living bees in with another colony."

"Won't they kill each other, Grandfather? You told me once that every colony has a special smell, and stranger bees may not go into other hives."

"That is often so. But look, you have brought sugar water. I will sprinkle it onto the little pile of living bees, the ones that no longer have a queen. Their wings will stick together, and I will sweep them with a feather into another hive. When the guards notice the new bees, they will start buzzing and want to attack the intruders and sting them. But as soon as the frontline warriors realize how sweet the new bees are, they will lick the wings, legs, heads, and bodies. In that way they will get to like the left-behind creatures and will keep them in their hive as beloved sisters." How miraculous! that enemies could become friends with just a sweet drink.

Grandfather now opens the back window of another hive box. He sprinkles the queenless bees with the sugar water, using a little brush and then uses a feather to sweep them into the neighboring hive box. Immediately the guard bees descend on the sugar-coated bees. But instead of stingers, they welcome them with little licking tongues. The sugar-bodies and wings are tirelessly caressed with sucking tongues.

After the window is closed and the insulation pad put back, Grandfather grips the shovel of dead bees. He pokes around with his finger until he finds the dead queen. "Look, Oliver, the bee mother lived for five years in this dry vessel." He puts the dead queen into the boy's hand. Grandfather shakes the other dead bees from the shovel into a furrow in the ground where he makes compost for the garden and slowly layers a little mound of dirt on top with his shoe.

Oliver gazes at the precious body-shell of the dead queen, counts the rings on the long body, and strokes the stiff wings. Finally, he takes it and goes back up to the house. He has a box hidden underneath the eaves of the roof where he keeps birds' nests, moss, and glittering rocks. He lays the royal body gently into a nest, and, after looking at it once again, finally closes the lid to the box.

THE LIFE OF A QUEEN

"How long does a queen live, Grandfather?" Oliver asks as they are sitting together in the living room one evening.

"Their lifespan is about three to five years. You are already as old as two queen lives put together. In the summer the honeybees live just five or six weeks. Only in the winter does their long hibernation keep them alive from the fall to the spring."

"Grandfather, tell me everything you know about the bees and the queen. I want to hear about it every day starting right now. I don't have to go to bed yet."

Grandfather begins, "To the bees, the queen is the most beloved thing in the world. There are always a few handmaidens close to her to help her because, strangely enough, the queen will take no food by herself. Even if she is very hungry and happens to walk by a big drop of honey, she will not take anything from it. But the servants watch out for her very well. As soon as they notice that the queen wants some food, they dive into a honey container with their proboscises. They carry the honey in their bodies for a while and transform it into a very delicate juice.

After that they bring it to the queen and put it on her tongue as if they were using a spoon.

"Just think, Oliver, there are some spring days when the queen lays more than a thousand eggs in a single day. Bees grow from those eggs just like flowers sprout from the seeds that we plant in the ground. As the bee mother grows older and older, she lays fewer and fewer eggs. She begins to have trouble moving, and the colony becomes smaller and weaker. When that happens, the bees don't fly outside so happily every morning, and they bring hardly any nectar home. It is as if they sense that the time will come soon when their dear queen must die.

"One day, in her language, she gives the bees a sign that she will lay a queen egg. Her servants immediately call for the best building mistresses of the hive and command them to build a chamber for a special queen egg. You have probably already seen how the bees have dark and light rings on their abdomens. They sweat out small, yellow disks from between those rings. The disks are their building blocks. They are called wax. Actually, it is honey that has been transformed. With such yellow wax disks, they now begin to build a chamber for the queen egg. As soon as the building has progressed to the size of the top of an acorn, the queen lays an egg inside. Afterward, the servants go and touch it with their feelers and are very happy about it.

"But the master builders have to hurry now and finish the queen's cradle. They lengthen the cell enough for a grown queen to have room inside. But they leave an opening at the bottom. Only on the third day does something begin to stir inside the egg. A tiny little worm crawls out. The best nurturing bees take care of it. They surround the little queen worm with sweet juice. Others group themselves around the chamber and nestle against the chamber walls so that the royal offspring stays very warm. The little worm begins to grow, and in five days it is so big that it fills nearly the whole chamber.

"Again, the wax builders are called in, this time to put a lid on the opening and seal the chamber, because in eight days the miraculous transformation that will turn the fat, white larva into a queen will take place. It is just like when a hard bud blossoms into a beautiful flower. Every little crack in the chamber must be sealed. Even the bees may not be spectators of this miracle.

"You see, Oliver, inside the dark chamber the sunny soul of the new queen comes in and takes its place inside the dark body. From the slimy worm, it slowly forms a head, thorax, and abdomen. The feelers stretch out, the legs have joints, and, at the very end, the tender wings are woven. After the queen's soul has formed the new body to the minutest detail, she quietly tries to move her legs and wings. Her head wobbles. She tries to stick out her little tongue. Yes, she even makes an effort to crawl around in the narrow chamber.

"The nurturing bees can hear her from the outside. They have been waiting day and night for the new queen to stir. They diligently begin to gnaw away the lid to free the young queen and greet her. They have great happiness and excitement when she slips out of the chamber. Some bees hand her honey juice, and some brush her wings.

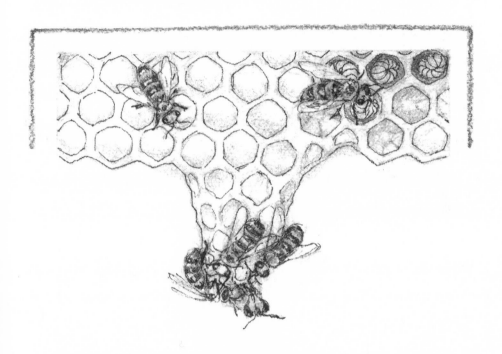

"A new mood comes over the hive as if a new, radiant Sun has risen while the old one is being extinguished. The old queen cannot stay much longer in her shaky, weak body. I have heard it told that sometimes she goes to the young queen in order to receive the sting of death. The new queen supposedly sticks her stinger between the abdomen rings, and so ends the life of the tired queen. If that happens, the servants take the body of the old mother and carry it to the exit. From the landing board, they fly with the royal body to a flowering meadow to make her a grave. Then they hurry back to serve the new queen as loyally as they served the old one.

"Other beekeepers have seen it that an old and a new queen will often live peacefully together for awhile in the hive. If the old one feels that her strength is leaving, she undertakes the flight of death to the meadow by herself. It has also happened that she is found alone and dead in a corner of the hive where she crawled to die. So silently and inconspicuously does a queen bee go to her death, without any complaint.

"But the royal strength and knowledge of the old bee mother does not die. It lives on in the young queen. That is why a new queen knows how to take care of everything without having to learn it. The colony will soon be fresh and chipper again. Yes, one could say that it has been given a new lease on life."

THE SUN FLIGHT

One afternoon, as Oliver is spending some time in front of the bee house, he sees the honeybees flying back and forth energetically from somewhere close by. Suddenly he is startled to see two or three really large, thick-bodied bees come strongly buzzing out of a nearby flight entrance and fly unsteadily into the distance. Oliver rushes up to Grandfather in the workshop and reports about the bees that look enormous to him, probably due to their loud buzzing.

"Those are male bees. They are called drones," Grandfather explains. "They are peculiar creatures. On warm days they fly out into the fields, but not to suck flower nectar. They are not able to do that. They buzz around in the sunny air and sit on a leaf or a warm rock when they are tired. If they get hungry, they return to the hive and let the caretaker bees pour honey juice into them like they were little bee babies. Then they laze around, look into the honey cells, and soon want to eat again."

"Don't the other bees get angry when those sluggards sit around, get in the way, and eat the honey?" Oliver asks.

"No, Oliver. As long as the meadow flowers are not mowed down, they will patiently feed the fat drones, and the drones become round and glossy from the sweet juice. There is only one time in their lives that the queen flies out into the world — with the drones. A short time after the queen hatches, she says something like this to the drones, 'Today I am flying out into the world, high into the sky, as high as my wings will carry me toward the Sun. You drones will escort me on my sun flight. The one who can climb the highest with me shall become my consort.'

"As the queen leaves through the exit hole, a train of drones follows her. While they are climbing higher, the fattest and laziest are soon left behind. The queen goes higher and higher in powerful circles. Fewer and fewer drones are able to follow her. But the last one left will fly with the queen high into the sunny sky. The queen climbs to this height in the blue sky only one time in her life. It is said that this is her wedding day.

"After she has flown wide circles in the sky, the queen suddenly dives toward the ground like a shooting star. She leaves the drones and, with sure instincts, finds her way back to her hive. The bees receive her with joyful buzzing. But the drone that was left by the queen never finds his way back to the hive.

"Towards summer the time comes when the farmers mow the blooming meadows and dry the grass for hay. The honeybees bring smaller drops of nectar home to the hive. The drones would like to suck away all the nectar from the gatherers' proboscises right away. But now the worker bees' patience with the lazy louts has come to an end. Finally one day they refuse food to the fat gobblers and force them out of the way. The drones have never learned to feed themselves, so they now become distressed and weak from hunger. The worker bees crowd out the once-plump drones. Even sometimes guards and builder bees attack them. They nip at their feet and bodies, tug on their wings, and chase them out of the fly hole. This is called the slaughter of the drones. The drones cannot really defend themselves. They do not even have stingers. There is such a buzzing and chasing going on in the hive, one might think it is a late swarm. It is strangely funny to see how the drones whirl around the landing board and absolutely do not want to leave. The bees quickly form another attack. Often two bees will grab a drone by its wings and carry it far off into a field. In the evening, the guards will not let even one drone back into the hive. Finally, they crawl off into the meadow grass with their distinctive droning, buzzing sound, and, half asleep, breathe their last in the dew of the cool night."

The Hive Swarms

The next evening, Grandfather continues telling the boy about the bees. "Oliver, you have heard how the old queen silently gives over the care of the hive to the young queen. Today you shall hear how it happens that there is a new bee colony. The meadows and trees are now in full bloom. So there could be a swarm very soon. If so, you will have to help me, so listen to what goes on.

"In May, when all the flowers on the trees are in bloom, the queen lays many, many eggs in one day. Now the hive grows very quickly, so much that there is hardly any place left for all the bees in the hive. Sometimes it happens that the worker bees will build one or several queen chambers at this time, and the queen lays an egg in each one. But since she is neither old nor weak, she will not get the sting of death from the new queen when she is hatched. But two queens cannot stay in one hive.

"As the sixteenth day approaches, all of the bees in the hive become more and more restless. The queens shine on them like two lamps, and they do not quite know which one they should follow. They begin swirling around in the box, buzzing loudly, and wildly running into each other. Some of them buzz, 'We will follow the old queen. Let us take some honey for the trip!'

"The others call out, 'We are not coming. We will stay with the young queen!'

"In all the bluster, suddenly there is a delicate, but clear, tooting sound: tu, tu, tu … The old queen is trumpeting. That is her signal that she wants to leave the hive. It is as if she is asking: 'Who is coming with me?' The bees frantically race to the exit, 'We are coming to the sunny festival!' Outside, they buzz and swirl around in the air, and wait for the queen. All at once, she appears on the landing board, surrounded by thousands. She takes off, and maybe directs the flight toward the outermost branch of the pear tree that stands in the yard. The bees roar after her like they were on a wild chase.

"As soon as the queen sets down on the branch, a fiery storm of bees rains down on her. They surround and enclose their mother. Bees hang on bees—hundreds, thousands are entwined around her, until the air has cleared, the bees are calm, and the cluster hangs off the branch like a heavy bunch of grapes. Every so often, a straggler flies up; usually it is a gatherer that was out in the field when the swarm started out. Now she has come home and wants to remain loyal to the old queen. She sets herself down on the swarm together with her little yellow pollen leggings.

"About half of the bees have remained in the old hive. Peace gradually returns there also. After a few days, the young queen slips out of her chamber cell.

"But what shall we do with the colony in the pear tree? We will get a box, a board, and two rods. We will lay all of these things under the tree. Then I will carefully stand a ladder against the branch where the swarm is, and be careful that the swarm bunch is not jolted. I will climb the ladder with the box and hold it under the hanging swarm. When I give the branch a strong blow, the swarm will fall into the box. The bees will already be very restless inside the box, but, even so, I will quickly descend the ladder with it. Once I am under the tree, I will put it on the board with the opening on the bottom. Inside, the queen will go quickly to the upper wall. Because the box has been put on rods, the bees that were lost during the shaking can find their way back inside through the holes between the board and the box.

"If we had not gotten the queen, then the whole swarm would fly out again and surround her anew. But, with the queen inside, they will gather together in the wooden box, and the box can be carried down into the cool cellar in the evening. The young colony will become very quiet. Even the softest buzzing will stop. The thousands of bees hang on each other, unmoving and stiff, as if they were a single, large bee body whose heart is the queen. They are fortunate that the queen was not lost during the flight out, and they sink into a deep sleep. Only the next evening will they be given a new hive box in the bee house.

"During their long rest in the darkness of the cellar, the bees in the swarm brew up a new perfume that will bind them all in new friendship, love and work. From now on it will hold them all tightly together. Now they will not mistakenly enter the old hive where they used to live, but rather will stay in their new hive as a young, fresh colony."

THE BOY IN THE SWARM

Curious, Oliver asks Grandfather to tell him more about the bee swarms. Grandfather tells him about the following incident:

"One time there was a boy, a gardener's son, standing close to a bee house, watching the bees flying around. It was the time of year for swarms. From one of the hive boxes came loud swishing and buzzing, and just then a part of the hive was sent out to swarm with the old queen. The gardener's son watched from very close by how more and more whirling bees were storming out of the fly hole. Finally, the queen appeared and took off from the landing board.

"Now, this queen was older and her wings were not so strong any more. So, she flew right to the side of the boy's head. The boy's father was working a little further away in the garden at this time. The boy had just yelled in a loud voice, 'Father, the bees are swarming!' when he was overtaken by the powerfully buzzing swarm that was intent on surrounding their queen.

"Fortunately, in that moment, the boy remembered something his father had often told him: 'Do not ever lash out against the bees or try to smack them away from you!' So, the boy stood there, motionless. His father rushed over and saw the child covered in bees. 'Close your eyes and your mouth!' he called to the boy. 'Breathe through your nose and don't move. I will get some water to cool off the bees, and then I will catch them. Stay still!'

"While his father was getting the necessary tools together, an impressive clump of bees was hanging sideways from the boy's head clear down to his shoulder. When his father returned, he dunked a brush into the water bucket and sprinkled a cool wetness over the swarm. The swarm slowly started to calm down. This whole time, the boy stood there like a tree trunk, stiff and rigid. With one hand, the father put a box underneath the hanging bunch and grabbed the boy's hair on the bee-free side of his head. When he gave the boy's head a firm jerk, the swarm fell into the box – queen and all! The bees still on the boy's shoulder also flew into the box that his father had now put to one side on the ground.

" 'Open your eyes, and come here!' his father cried happily to his boy. The boy carefully opened his eyes and slowly turned his head. When he realized that no more bees were clinging to him, he started cheering and ran to his father. 'Not one bee stung me!' he cried.

" 'Because you stood there so quietly,' his father said, and patted him on the shoulder. 'You're really something, you know that?'

"Later in the afternoon, as the two were working in the garden, the father let the hoe fall all of a sudden, and said, 'Listen, my boy, later in your life, if you ever find yourself in danger, just think back to the way you stood calmly in the bee swarm, and how fear did not get the best of you. I am proud of you!' After that, they continued hoeing the garden, father and son."

Swarming Day

Just about noontime on a warm day in May, Oliver is getting ready to do some work in the garden. All at once he hears loud, high buzzing sounds coming from the bee house. When he goes to look, he sees a whirling cloud of bees. *That must be a swarm,* he thinks, and he hurries up to the house to tell Grandfather.

Grandfather comes with swifter steps than usual to the bee house, stands with the boy to the side of the house, and says, "Now, pay attention to where they fly off, hopefully not up and away." The queen must have just flown out because the swarming group moves away from the little house and buzzes around a plum tree. The swarm begins to bunch on the lowest branch.

"They're going to stay on the plum tree," Oliver whispers excitedly. The bees are beginning to cluster, and the tree branch bends down deeply from the weight of the large colony.

"Go to the kitchen and get a plate with a little flour on it," Grandfather tells Oliver. "We want to tell exactly from which hive the swarm came." Oliver wonders how the flour can help, but he is soon back with what Grandfather requested. Only a few straggler bees still fly around the tree, so Grandfather and Oliver can take their time looking at the swarm.

"Look, Grandfather, some of the bees are carrying their little leggings of pollen. They must have come from the field and didn't even have time to unload at the hive."

Grandfather takes the plate of flour closer to the swarm, and says, "Go over to the bee house, Oliver. I am going to take a few bees from the swarm and put them on the plate of flour. They will become white all over and return to their old hive to get cleaned up. You watch like a hawk and let me know which hive the white bees fly into. Then we will know exactly which one is the mother hive."

The boy eyes the landing boards with a sharp gaze. Suddenly a white bee crawls over the landing board that is second from the front. A second and third bee follow. The flour-legged ones quickly disappear inside, all through the same opening. Oliver calls out, "I saw them! They went into the hive second closest to the front."

"That's what I thought," says Grandfather. "Come here and get me a bucket of water. Now we will catch the swarm. I'll get the other tools. I don't need a ladder because the branch is hanging so low." Soon a board is lying on the ground with a box on top. Grandfather dips a brush into the bucket of water and sprinkles the swarm with it in order to calm it down completely. Now he holds the box underneath the swarm. A hefty shake and the colony falls into the box. Above the board, Grandfather turns the box, teeming with bees, and arranges the pieces of wood so that some space remains between the box and the board. During this process, Oliver steps over to the side. He is amazed that the bees do not sting, and that everything is happening so peacefully. Only a few bees fly off, but they soon find their way back and crawl inside the box. "Now they should stay in the shade under the tree for the rest of the day. In the evening we will carry them down to the cellar."

"Why is it that the bees don't sting during a swarm?" the boy asks.

"Before they fly out," Grandfather replies, "they drink in a lot of sweet honey for the trip, and that puts them in a good mood. Besides, swarming day is a joyous occasion for the bees. Only if it is hot and humid weather do they sometimes become testy. More than a few beekeepers have experienced that."

Often throughout the afternoon Oliver goes to the box and observes how single bees fly out sometimes and others fly in.

Before it gets dark, Grandfather carries the board and box into the cellar. Oliver holds a lantern so there will be no accident on the stairs. Before they leave the cellar, Oliver puts his ear to the box and hears a fine, barely noticeable, tender buzzing noise. He quietly whispers, "Good night, little escapees. I'm going to bed now, too."

How the Swarm Comes out of the Cellar and into a New Hive

That night and the next day the swarm rests in the quiet of the cellar. The next evening Grandfather gently carries the box with the sleeping colony back up the cellar stairs. He has readied a hive box for them in the bee house and has hung up some honeycomb in it. He takes away the door at the back of the hive box and, with a heavy clap on the side of the box, the swarm pours through the opening to the inside of their new hive. All of them move in, with the queen going in last.

After all the bees are inside, the glass panel at the back of the hive is set in, the box closed, and the colony happily buzzes around its queen in its new home. The wax-making bees immediately begin to sweat out abundant amounts of wax because a new hive must be built. The builder bees form fresh cells for the offspring and honey. Right away the queen lays large numbers of eggs. The life and times of the new colony have begun.

In the morning the bees crawl out onto their new landing board for the first time. After their long sleep in the cellar, they have forgotten where they used to fly in and out. "How do they find their way back here if they fly to far-off meadows?" Oliver asks. "Why don't they get mixed up about their entrance and fly into another hive?"

"That is very curious," Grandfather replies. "You have surely seen bees on the landing board that lift up their abdomens and whir very fast with their wings. These are the scent bees. All bees have the ability to release a fine aroma from the back of their abdomens. Every colony has a different odor. The bees can recognize the smell of their own colony from even a great distance. The smell shows them the way to their hive as if it were a fine thread leading them to the right entrance. Bees can see only dimly with their eyes. The world swims before them in delicate colors. But if every landing board is painted a different color, then it is easier for them to find their own entrance, and then they never fly to another hive."

THE BEE SWARM IN THE FOREST

The same evening the swarm moved into their new hive, Oliver sits with Grandfather in the living room. Grandfather says, "Today I will tell you what happens if the queen doesn't fly to the next tree when they swarm. Sometimes, she will lead her colony far away from the bee house into a distant forest where no beekeeper can find them and catch them.

"The May nights often bring a cold frost. Let's say a queen flies from the bee house with her swarm around midday, further and further over the fields, until finally she lands on a beech tree in the forest. The bees buzz after her in a long train and group around her on the tree branch. There hangs the buzzing bunch high in the crown of the tree. No beekeeper will be able to find them and give them a new hive in the bee house. Yes, even if someone happens to walk under the tree, he will probably think that the clump of bees is just an outgrowth of the branch.

"The evening arrives. When the Sun goes down, a cool wind blows through the branches. The outermost bees become stiff. Darkness brings still greater cold. The clear, starry night allows a frost to spread over the land. The outside of the swarm bunch becomes completely stiff. But in the middle, where the queen is protected, it remains warm as breath.

"A new day begins and the swarm begins to stir. As the first sunbeams bring new life, a few of the stiffened outside bees fall to the forest floor. Many bees now fly in all directions into the forest trying to find a protected place, somewhere that can serve as a new hive for the colony. They crawl between rocks, under tree roots, and into holes in the ground. One of the searchers thinks she has found a secure hollow in a tree trunk, but the entrance only leads to a narrow mouse hole. Maybe another bee happens upon a foxhole. The queen waits in vain up in the beech tree. The messengers return in the evening with no good news.

"However, there is one loyal, old bee that continues the search after sundown. She would rather die in the frost than return to her queen without good news. She has just come to an ancient tree trunk and crawls up it. About halfway up, she finds a round opening. She slips inside and soon realizes that she has discovered a hollow tree. Years ago there must have been sparrows nesting there because the rotten wood has been cleanly pecked out. The old bee sister now flies like the wind back to her colony in the beech tree. She presses her way through hundreds of sister bees in order to report to the queen about her find. The news travels like wildfire through the swarm: 'We have a house! We have a house!'

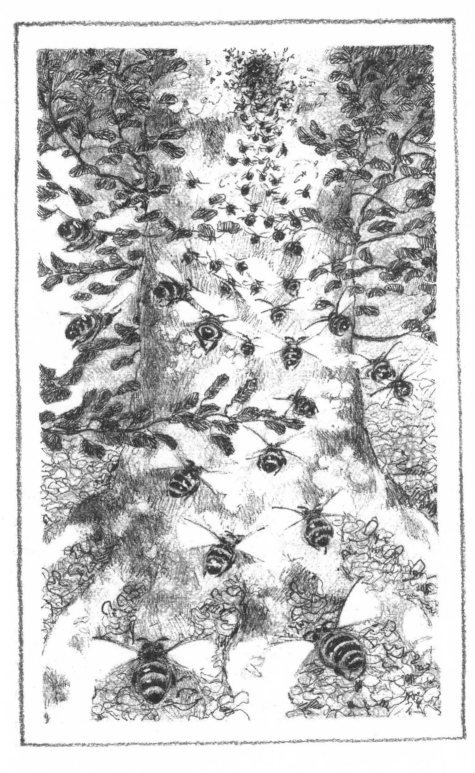

"Already the queen's call can be heard, giving the signal to leave. The hanging colony comes to life. A whirring sound fills the air until the queen appears and, along with the loyal discoverer as a guide, leads the flight to the hollow tree. The bees stream into the opening and are so happy about the warm, snug tree house. This new hive has only one problem: The entrance is very wide open.

"But nobody thinks about the winter now. Everyone is joyful about the protective tree. Right away the wax-making bees go into a deep corner, huddle close together to stay warm, and sweat until the first little yellow disks appear from between the rings on the underside of their abdomens. The builder bees quickly grab the fresh wax with the small pincers on their mandibles and begin to build their rows of cells, starting at the top of the hollow and building all the way down to the bottom.

"When the earliest bees arise with the Sun and fly out to the flowers, the queen lays the first eggs in the tree hive. When the gatherers return, enough cells have been built for them to put the golden drops and the pollen inside.

"And so it continues like this in the summer months. The whole hollow of the tree is built up with chambers and cells. With the autumn getting closer, almost all of the cells are filled with honey. The guards that watch over the entrance, and prevent thieving wasps from getting in, sense that the time is coming that will paralyze bees and their wings. A cool autumn wind blows the leaves from the trees. The guards can hardly stand the cold that creeps inside. They call to the builder bees, 'Fill up the opening with wax!'

"The builder bees go to the wax makers and request: 'Give us wax! We have to narrow the entrance. We want to build a winter door!'

" 'It's about time you were showing up,' the wax makers say. 'It's probably already too cold for us to sweat out much wax. Let us try and see if it works.' They huddle up close together to get the necessary warmth, but only a few tiny, little disks come out from between their rings. That is not enough. So, the bees fly out to look for some tree sap. They knead it together with some wax and build a door with it. They leave the opening only big enough so that enough fresh air can flow inside for the bees to breathe in the winter.

"From then on it becomes quieter in the hollow tree. With the first snowflakes, the winter hibernation of the bee colony begins. And, if the winter is not too terribly severe, the hive remains intact until spring, when it awakens to new life. I have heard it told that a wild beehive will awaken in the middle of the winter on Christmas Eve and make a delicate buzzing sound. It sounds like angels singing: 'Glory to God in the Highest, Peace on Earth…' I would like to hear that once, wouldn't you, Oliver!?"

When Grandfather finishes his story, Oliver asks, "Are there very many wild beehives in the forests?"

"No, they are very rare. They usually cannot survive our cold winters."

"Then how do the bumblebees and wasps do it? They don't get a hive given to them by people."

"It is like this: In the autumn the wasps and bumblebees all die except the queens. But the queens crawl in somewhere deep into the ground and sleep the winter away. In the spring they found new colonies."

How the Bees Divide Up
Their Work

We have heard about the various tasks which the bees carry
out as caretakers, wax makers, builders, guards, and honey
gatherers. But how do they care for all the different tasks? It
happens like this:

When the young bees have just slipped out of their cells, in
which they have grown for twenty-one days, caretakers come
around and stroke them, clean, and brush them. They also
get their first nourishment offered from the proboscises of the
caretakers. Then the new bees just stand around casually and
do not really understand what is to be done in all of the activity.

But soon, the older bees come and fetch them. They are
taken to the chambers where the eggs and white larvae are,
and the older ones command them in bee language, "Stay here
quietly and keep the brood warm with your bodies. You shall
do this until the third day." The new bees obediently sit there,
and from time to time they get some honey from the caretakers.
From the fourth day on they are allowed to give the little worms

and larvae honey juice. They mix in a little pollen for the older larvae. So, they become caretakers as well. This work allows them to circulate around the hive.

One day the new bees, now around seven days old, discover the light at the opening of the entrance to the hive. "Oh, what is that? What is shining so brightly?" They briskly crawl toward the light.

But the gate guards gruffly buzz, "What are you doing here, young ones? You may not fly out into the world until the twentieth day. Go back inside!"

The seven-day-olds swiftly return to where they were before. They probably think: *It must be a beautiful wonderland outside where our older sisters fly and find the sweet nectar and golden pollen.* They ask an elder bee about it.

The elder explains kindly, "The outside world is filled with star cups the way our hive is filled with wax cells. The bright Sun shines from the sky into all the cups. They ring like delicate bells, and from these Sun sounds flows the sweet-smelling nectar."

"What is the Sun?" the young bees ask.

"That is our big sister in the sky, the queen of the world," the old bee replies. "Tomorrow, go once more to the guards and ask them if you may stand just outside on the landing board for a little while. Then you will be able to see our mother in the sky."

The next day, the eight-day-olds again go towards the bright door. This time the guards let them pass. The young bees stand on the landing board, blinded by the brilliance of the sunny day.

There are soft, singing tones coming from the meadow. The sunbeams make the bees' wings flutter with joy. They hardly notice when they are suddenly lifted into the air. They sway up and down in front of the landing board a hundred times, drinking in the fullness of the light. Tired from their sunny game, they finally slip back inside the hive and resume loyally caring for the brood. But they can hardly wait for the day when they may fly freely into the sunny world.

On the tenth day the young bees are required to strip off the pollen from the legs of the incoming bees and press it into the wax cells with their heads. Chamber after chamber is filled with sun flour. But they also help to fill up other cells with nectar. If a nectar carrier bee comes by, she lets the juice flow out of her proboscis in little drops. The younger bees suck it in and fill up the cells with it.

Around the eighteenth day, the young bees sweat out wax disks and diligently work to finish new cells or build wax lids for the cells that are already full. The strongest among them may go and watch at the entrance at this time. When it is hot and humid in the hive on summer days, rows of the young bees stand at the entrance and flap their wings very fast. That is how they fan out the hot air from the hive. Fresh air comes inside and cools the colony.

Sometimes a greedy wasp will fly around the hive, trying to get in to steal honey. He will set down unnoticed onto the landing board and hurry to the entrance as if he were a bee. But the guard bees recognize his distinct and different scent. They angrily attack the would-be robber. A whirling fight begins. No matter how the wasp bites and stings, it is pulled by its legs and wings, and thrown out in a high arc over the landing board. The poison from the guards' stings can long be felt in the wasp's body. It lies in the grass all curled up for a while. "He won't come again," the sentinels buzz, as they resume their places behind the hive entrance.

Flight into the World

The twentieth day finally arrives. This is the long-awaited day when the young bees will be allowed to fly out into the world for the first time.

The not-so-young bees appear on the landing board with the early morning Sun. Such enchanting aromas and singing colors greet them from the meadow. The bees fly up. A thousand sparkling sun drops glitter underneath in the dewy grass, and a sea of fragrant star cups blazes and resounds in the fiery morning light. From the garden comes the solid, rich tone of the tulips and, next to them, the tender song of the violets and forget-me-nots. From all the meadows comes the bubbly chiming of the dandelions.

"Yellow Sun, I am coming to you!" one of the bees cries, and dives into the golden flower. At once she is completely covered in pollen. She busily brushes and kneads the pollen into golden leggings, and then flies on to the next dandelion. Once the bees have chosen a particular kind of flower, they remain true to it for the entire time they are flying that day. Often they will visit only one kind of flower for several days in a row.

For its first flight, another bee turns to the quiet forget-me-not. The little drop that the sky-blue cup offers is very tiny, but a hundred such tiny drops add up to one normal-sized.

The blooms on a cherry tree are fully open from the previous night. The nectar really flows! Early in the morning the first bee comes to that bright, flower kingdom. Her body becomes big and plump, and she flies, heavily-laden, back to the hive. She has hardly handed over the juicy nectar when she begins to dance in the middle of the group – once to the right, one rotation to the left. Again, she bends and nods her head and shakes her body around. What kind of awesome moves are these? It is the cherry blossom dance. Other bees notice the dancer, and they understand the message. As this bee gets ready to dance out of the hive, a group of about twelve nectar gatherers flies out with her to the cherry tree. Cheerfully, they buzz around in the blossoms, return heavy with nectar to the hive, and all dance the cherry blossom dance again. This time a large group of over a hundred bee sisters follows them back to the tree. It is often the bees from a single hive will fill up a cherry tree with their buzzing early in the morning.

If a bee from another hive happens to find the same nectar palace, she will go and tell her sisters bees. Honeybees do not bicker over nectar like dogs over a bone or people over money or property. If a flower is occupied, a newcomer bee will fly over it and leave her sister to have the nectar. One never sees bees fighting over a nectar cup. The bees have a special dance for practically all of the nectar flowers that they use to call their sisters. They have similar dances for pollen as well.

When the Sun goes down in the evening, the air quickly becomes cooler. Any bee that does not make the return flight in time will stiffen in the dew of the night. Or she might crawl into a crack in the ground when her wings will not work any more, thus preserving her life for another day in the protection of the Earth. Sometimes one finds a dead bee in a flower chalice. That is because when their time has come, the old bees may die right in the middle of their work in the meadow, and go to their graves among the luminous petals.

How the Bees Propagate Fruit

The cherry tree in the yard in front of the bee house usually blooms later than all the other trees in the area. Oliver has heard from Grandfather that the bees help to propagate fruit, and that without bees the fruit trees would be practically empty at harvest time. *I wonder how that happens,* Oliver thinks, and he asks Grandfather to tell him about it sometime.

Now the two of them are standing by the cherry tree and the first blossoms have opened. Grandfather pulls a branch down toward him just as a bee lands on it. The bee is so intent on her task that she is not disturbed. Grandfather whispers, "Look! It's a pollen gatherer. She is busy going at the golden, mealy stamen of the flower. You see, the fine dust sticks to all the little hairs on her body. Now look at the inside of the cherry blossom and you will see a little green stem in the middle of the golden stamen. On the top is a protrusion. That is actually the delicate mouth of the blossom. When the bee crawls into the blossom, she rubs off a little pollen dust onto the mouth of the flower, without even noticing she has done so. At once the little mouth begins to suck in the golden pollen. In this way the pollen gets into the green nodes at the bottom of the flower cup and brings the fire of the Sun inside. The node now begins to grow. The flower wilts and when it falls, a tiny, green cherry appears. If no pollen penetrated inside to the green nodes, then they would spoil when the blossoms wilt. In that case, nothing could bring that tree to produce cherries."

Grandfather lets go of the branch. But Oliver asks another question, "What about the cherry pits?"

"Before it becomes hard," Grandfather explains, "the Sun's energy that has slipped in with the pollen also works and weaves in the pit. It fires the cherry thoroughly from the inside, and the fruit really swells up. The outer Sun provides energy and ripens the green fruit into sweet, juicy cherries. The bitter part is loosened and goes inside the cherry to the kernel. If you open one up in the summer, you can taste it for yourself!" Grandfather goes up to the house and leaves Oliver standing under the tree.

Suddenly, Oliver has a thought: *Last autumn, didn't Mother sew little sacks out of old net curtains to hang around the largest bunches of grapes so the bees and wasps couldn't hollow out the fruit? Couldn't I take such a sack and tie it around a branch of the cherry tree that hasn't bloomed yet? Yes, I will do it! Then the few blossoms under the netting will bloom, no bee will be able to pollinate them, and I will see clearly if what Grandfather has told me is really true.* Right away Oliver runs up to the attic. Nothing is hidden from him there. He knows exactly where Mother keeps things. He looks for a sack that does not have any holes or tears.

Back at the tree, he chooses the tip of a budding branch that does not yet have any open blossoms. He puts the little net sack over it and winds some string around it at the back to hold the netting in place. No bee will be able to get in.

Oliver very proudly shows his invention to Grandfather in the evening. Grandfather checks the string to see that it is tightly wound and finds everything in order. "Maybe you will become a people doctor someday since you're already good at doctoring on the trees," he laughs. A few days later the flowers in the little sack bloom, but no bee can slip through the netting.

Fourteen days later the cherry tree is in full bloom. Thousands of little green cherries appear where the blossoms have wilted and fallen away. Oliver calls Grandfather to come and see. He wants Grandfather to be there when he takes the little net sack away. The boy unwinds the string while Grandfather holds the branch. As soon as the netting is off, the dry blossoms and stems fall to the ground. A few still hang loosely on the branch, but they are also dry.

As he is closely examining the branch, Oliver suddenly sees three beautifully formed little green cherries underneath the dead stems. "Look at that, Grandfather. Something's not right. A bee certainly couldn't have gotten inside."

The old man winked, and said, "It wasn't a bee, but a gentleman that you hadn't thought of. Try and guess!"

"Then it was an ant!"

"No!"

"A little beetle?"

"No, it is something that no bee possesses."

Oliver could not think what it could be.

"It was the wind. He blew through your net and deposited some cherry pollen inside these three blossoms. That is why people in the know speak of wind pollination and bee pollination. But, you can see what a poor showing the powerful wind makes against our industrious bees. Without our bees, there would be only a meager harvest."

When it is time to harvest the cherries, Oliver picks the three wind cherries. Mother eats one, Grandfather another, and Oliver munches down the third one himself.

Ants, Bees, and Butterflies

Have you ever seen how a nimble ant on its way through the meadow will climb a flower stem and go inside the bloom? Right away it begins to suck nectar from the base of the flower chalice. Take a good look at the ant and you will see how the shape of its body is related to that of a bee, even though the ant has no wings.

The ant colony lives in a dark hill. In narrow, dark passages and chambers, their eggs grow into larvae and then into ants, in a way similar to how it happens with bees. Their young even get nectar juice to drink. That is why the older ants also climb up to the flower cups. But watch out if a bee wants to land on a flower where an ant is biding its time. As soon as the ant notices the humming of wings, it turns and lifts itself up and begins to scratch in the air like a mean cat. The bee gets a shock when such a grimacing mug comes floundering toward it from the soft flower, and it quickly flies away. The ant thinks that since it took all the trouble to climb up the flower, then it must be a nectar garden for just itself alone.

After it has nipped a little more of the juice, an ant from another colony climbs up the flower stem. Unexpectedly, it appears inside the flower cup. BAM, POW! Such a fight breaks out. The stronger grabs the weaker by the throat and makes a swinging throw onto the ground below.

Along comes a butterfly, fluttering over the meadow, and gets close to the occupied flower. It sinks to the colorful crown in silent glides. But, oh no, scratching, scraping feet are already running toward it. The startled butterfly returns to the air and flies further on. No butterfly wishes to spar with an ant.

Finally, the little brown, scuttling ant has quenched its thirst for nectar. It happily walks back down to the ground. The flower is once again a friendly garden where bees and butterflies diligently work side by side, as sisters.

Honey Day

One day, after the linden tree blossoms have withered, Grandfather says to Oliver, "Today is honey day. Come with me to the bee house. You may help me gather the honey."

With care Grandfather assembles what he needs in the bee house: a bucket of water and a large chicken feather. Then he lights a few pieces of dry, rotten wood in a container and slowly gets it smoking with a small bellows. Oliver is in a very festive mood. Although he wants to ask why all of these things are important, he stands quietly behind Grandfather and silently wonders if a bee will sting him. He has heard that bees will sting more readily when honey is being taken away from them.

In the meantime, Grandfather opens a hive box, takes the smoke container, puffs two plumes of smoke through the hatch at the back of the hive, and closes it again. "You see, Oliver, the bees now think their neighborhood is on fire. They will hurry to the honey cells and suck themselves full in order to save as much as possible. When I open the box again and take out some of the honeycomb, they will not be angry because they have sucked in so much sweet honey into their bodies." He turns again to the box and takes away the back window pane. As he takes out one honeycomb, he sees it is covered all over with bees. Holding it over the box, Grandfather hits the wooden frame of the honeycomb with his strong fist. The honey-laden bees fall down like ripe plums when the tree is shaken. The ones that had not let go are gently swept back into the hive with the wet chicken feather.

So it goes from frame to frame and hive to hive. More honey is taken from the stronger colonies than from the weaker ones. There is nothing to take from the young swarm. But not all of the honey is taken from the bees. They need to keep a part of it for their winter rations.

"Grandfather, why do you move your hands so slowly? You are much more agile in the workshop."

"The bees don't like it at all if one is wriggling about. Then they begin to sting."

"Have any stung you today?"

"No, the weather is good. If there were a storm coming, I might have already been stung a dozen times."

Suddenly a bee flies into Oliver's hair and gets caught up in it. He quickly tries to brush it away with his hand, and it stings him on one finger. Grandfather smiles when he sees the shocked look on Oliver's face. "You should put on a straw hat like me. Your curly hair is like a spider web for the bees." Oliver feels a sharp pain in his finger. Grandfather continues, "Give me your hand. I'll pull out the stinger. You know, a bee stinger has barbs in it like a fish hook. That's why it stays stuck. Once a bee has used its stinger, it will die in a short time because when the barbs are pulled out, it injures the inside of the bee's body."

Grandfather presses out the little spike, shows it to Oliver and says, "It's not bad. In fact, a little bee venom is good for the blood. It helps get rid of bad fluids and makes the blood fresh and red. Go out to the meadow and rub the juice from a green leaf or some brown earth on the sting. That will take away the burning." Oliver follows the advice, and the burning sensation slowly passes.

After the harvest is carried up to the house, the wax lids that seal the honey cells have to be removed. Every filled honey cell is sealed with a wax lid by the builder bees. If these lids are left in place, the honey could not flow out. Grandfather places the comb into the honey extractor. As Oliver turns the wheel, he can hear how the honey inside the container smacks against the sides because of the fast-turning wheel. Soon a small tube is opened at the bottom of the extractor, and a golden fountain streams into the kettle waiting underneath. From time to time, when Oliver's arm grows tired from turning the wheel, he changes hands and quickly runs his index finger under the glistening fountain. The sweet gold tastes wonderful!

Grandfather notices that Oliver is a little over-zealous in getting in his licks, but he lets it go by. He figures it is not honey day every day. For supper Oliver's mother brings him a big piece of bread. He is allowed to hold it under the honey fountain. Suddenly the flow stops. Oh, no! Oliver had bent his head too far forward and the sticky honey has run into his hair. He will have to wash it in warm water before he can eat his honey bread.

In the evening, when all the work is finished, Grandfather dips the end of a match stick into the full kettle of honey, shows Oliver the little drop, and says, "Look at this little drop. What do you think? How many flowers does a bee have to visit to get one such drop?"

Oliver thinks for a moment and answers, "About ten or twenty!"

Grandfather's face becomes serious as he slowly and almost solemnly replies, "That is not the case. In this drop alone is the nectar from many thousands of flowers. The aromas of a large flower garden are contained in this single, golden pearl! People don't have a high enough regard for honey. One time I was a dinner guest at a family's home and honey was put on the table. The children left more honey sticking to their knives and plates than a hundred bees could gather in a day!" Now Oliver understands why Grandfather always wipes the honey knife two or three times on the last bite of bread, and why he always uses up the last little bit of honey on his plate.

From then on, when Oliver is given honey, he acts the same as Grandfather, and to the last drop he thinks about the aromatic flowers of the meadow, the Sun that allows them to grow, and the diligent bees, whose gift should be honored.

THE MOUSE IN THE BEEHIVE

One day Oliver finds an old beehive basket woven from straw in a dark corner of the attic. It is the kind that people used for hives in earlier times, and still today in many places. The boy takes it down to the workshop and shows it to Grandfather. Grandfather tells Oliver that he used such baskets years ago. And well he remembers once when a mouse had to do with such a hive basket. Oliver wants to hear about it, so Grandfather begins to tell the story:

"I used to have the straw baskets set up under the eaves of the barn. One day a mouse came sniffing around the baskets, looking for a place to build a nest that would be well protected from the cat. In all the looking around, she was very curious about the woven straw of the beehive. She began to gnaw and grate the straw with her sharp teeth. The opening went deeper into the basket until she happily realized there was a large chamber on the inside. With one jump the mouse was in the middle of the beehive.

"The guard bees noticed immediately that some sort of monster was trying to disturb the peace of the colony. They attacked the mouse and stung her on the back. Oh! She started running and dancing around wildly inside the basket. This action made the bees very agitated and angry. The sharp scent of the bee venom spread throughout the hive as a warning. In no time a large group of bees began covering the mouse's gray back with hard stings. The mouse was frantically squeaking and looking for an exit. But the entrance was too small. How was she to find the hole she had gnawed when she was jumping around so wildly? In a short time, the bee venom had driven all life from her limbs, and she lay dead on the wooden floor of the basket.

"Night came. The bees calmed down, and the next day they did not pay much attention to the dark mound, motionless on the floor. After a few days, however, the mound became very noticeable. In the honey-sweet atmosphere of the hive, the dead mouse began to spread a horrible stink of decay. When the bees returned to the hive from the lovely-smelling meadows, it seemed as if the foul air wanted to squeeze the soul from their bodies.

"What could be done? Shall the whole colony move out? It was not possible for the bees to carry out the mouse. It was much too big and heavy.

"In their great need, a saving idea went around the hive as if a light had been switched on. As if they had discussed it together, the wax bees hurriedly began to sweat out wax, and the builder bees began to erect a wall of wax and tree sap around the unfortunate mouse. The wall grew higher and higher until it arched over the mouse corpse. In the next few days the mausoleum was finished. Not one crack remained open. Just as the stink had spread throughout the hive, now the hive was permeated again with the golden honey scent of the colony.

"Autumn came, and with it the time that I, as a young beekeeper, took the last look inside the hives before winter. I lifted the straw basket off the wooden platform and saw a puzzling, brownish mound. I set the basket full of bees to one side and used a knife to loosen a piece of the wax covering. A gray pelt appeared. As I cut out more pieces of wax, I looked with amazement at the dead mouse. I kept my nose at a good distance as I scratched away the gray fur with a stick. I washed the board thoroughly for the bees and put the wise colony back on top of it.

"If the bees had not thought to build the mouse a burial chamber, I would have lost the hive. Either they would have been poisoned by the polluted air or they would have flown off to who knows where.

"I heard about another time a beekeeper found a small wax mound on the floor of a hive. When he cut it away, there appeared a dead snail. The bees had built a burial chamber for it, too."

Autumn Feeding

The plums are ripe on the tree in the yard. Oliver notices that when he picks up a plum that had fallen from the tree, there are bees sitting on it, and they have already made a hole in the tender, sweet fruit.

Today Oliver helps Grandfather put up a ladder against the plum tree. It is time to pick the fruit. While Grandfather sedately climbs the rungs, Oliver scrambles into the crown of the tree. The branches are jostled about and some of the overripe plums fall to the ground. The bees immediately start buzzing around in the leaves. They were banqueting on the fruit and are now looking for more. The boy calls from the tree, "Grandfather, the best fruit has been eaten into by the bees. Can't they stick with the flowers and let people have the fruit?"

Grandfather replies, "Look down at the fields. There is only late summer grass and no more nectar to be found. Even the garden flowers give very little in this dry time. That's why the bees take the sweet juice in the fruit. There's not much to be done about it. But it is a sign that I must begin with the feedings in the bee house. As soon as we have picked the plums, you may help me get the utensils ready that we will need and start the cleaning."

Oliver picks the fruit from the inner branches that is hard to reach from the ladder. The basket in the grass slowly fills up. After it is carried to the house, Grandfather takes the key to the bee house off of its peg. In a storage closet of the bee house are stored the little wooden boxes that serve as containers for the feedings. Grandfather explains, "See, one of these containers is put in the back of a hive. A bottle with sugar syrup is attached to this spigot. The bees can walk in and suck in the sweet juice from the edge of the little wooden container. Whatever juice they drink is replaced from the bottle. They go back to the honeycombs and fill the cells. As soon as a cell is full, the wax bees put a lid on it."

"Can't the bees carry in enough nectar for them to live on during the winter?" Oliver asks.

"Don't forget that we took out a lot of honey. But, yes, every hive has a good portion of its own honey left over. If the bees get too much sugar water they become weak and lethargic."

The required utensils are washed up in the spring-water fountain, and the bottles are fetched from the cellar and given a good rinsing. After the containers have dried in the Sun, Oliver carries them, as well as the bottles, to the bee house.

In the evening, as a big kettle of water simmers in the kitchen, Grandfather brings in the sugar. He takes some herbs out of a jar and throws them into the simmering water. He holds the jar under Oliver's nose. Oliver can clearly recognize the smell of chamomile, which he drank once as tea when he had a stomach ache. "Do the bees get tummy aches, too?" he asks, full of amazement.

Grandfather laughs, "No, that is not why I add the chamomile. The mild aroma of the chamomile mixes with the sugar water, and its flower energy goes into the sugar. The bees can take in the sugar water much easier that way, and it tastes almost as good as honey to them."

When it is dark the two carry the sweet beverage down to the bee house. Oliver holds a lantern to light the path. He knows that one should not feed the bees as long as it is daylight. The bees would get too excited if they suddenly got so much sweet juice. It has happened that when a hive has emptied their sugar water container, the next day the bees will have something like a sugar high, and perhaps storm into another hive that still has sugar water, to steal it from them. Naturally, the other hive will defend itself against the attack. A bee battle can ensue in which hundreds of bees are killed. That is why one feeds them after dark, when they do not fly out any more.

The feeding containers are already placed in the hives. The bottles are all filled. Bottle after bottle is tipped up into the containers, and, after a short time, a delicate buzzing indicates that the bees have been attracted by the smell and are heading toward the sweet feed. Throughout the night they carry the tea to their honey cells.

The next day the bottles and containers are empty. Now the hives will have two days of rest; then they will get another helping of sugar water. This will continue until they have enough winter rations, and the honeycomb in the furthest corner of the hive glistens with sweetness.

The cowbells are already ringing in the autumn meadow when Grandfather puts away the feeding utensils. Afterward, he begins to carefully put straw pillows on every hive. He makes sure that they are well-covered. Often he puts two pillows on top of each other; no hive should freeze in the winter cold. Outside, he pushes the panels of the flight entrances closer together, and says to Oliver, "Now the winter can come when it wants. My bees don't need to be afraid of it."

WINTER WANTS TO COME

The swallows have flown to warmer regions before winter, and the cherry tree has lost its yellow-red leaves. Although the sky is clear and blue, a bee seldom flies from the bee house into the cool, humid air. The herd is grazing the short grass in the meadow. The blooming summer is gone. Here and there a crocus shimmers in a green carpet of grass.

A bee has just taken off from the landing board. It searches the fields, searches the flowers, but no flower cups wave at her. Near the garden a fine whiff of perfume plays around her feelers. Like a lighted path, it leads her to a bush where the last asters are blooming. The late-flying bee happily flutters in the colorful star, but the little drop of nectar that she is able to carry home to the hive is meager and bitter. It shall be the last one.

The next day, no bees leave the hive any more. A hard frost has broken the verdant green of the trees. A white mantle of frozen dew lies over the land. The chiming bells of the cows have fallen silent. No guard bees are keeping watch at the hive entrance. They have withdrawn further inside. Early in the morning the beekeeper walks over the frozen blanket of grass down to the bee house to check once more that every hive entrance is open just enough. No biting wind will be able to blow through the narrow crack.

Inside the hive, the bees are now huddling up close together. The queen is surrounded and protected by her colony. It is the sun-warmth of the honey that radiates out from the bees. Whenever the calm warmth threatens to leave them, they crawl to a honey cell and drink in the summer nectar. The quiet glow returns immediately. Even when the winter comes, and sends the hardest frost, the beehives will stay warm.

The last leaves have been blown down. Crystal flakes fall steadily and cover the land in snow. The bees sink into their winter sleep. Warmed by the tender heat of the sun-honey, they dream of flower stars and the colorful suns in the summer meadow.

Maiden Worry and the Bees
A Legend Retold

Long ago there was a time on the Earth when people lived in much worry, fear, and grief. Mighty wars spread enormous misery, and brought disease and starvation. And when a new spring burst forth over the land, the people no longer found happiness in the beauty of the flowers and the singing birds. The colorful play of butterflies went unnoticed. In the evening if the people saw the Sun sink into glowing clouds, they remained unmoved by the sight. Troubled souls shut themselves off from the starry brilliance of the night. When the day ended, sleep also did not bring any real refreshment. More often than not, the people were frightened by bad dreams. The flowers in the meadows lost their lovely scent. Their petals wilted away even before they had fully bloomed. The crops in the fields produced less and less. Trees died, and many water springs dried up.

In such difficult times, hidden from human eyes, the figure of a grieving, virgin maiden goes throughout the land. Her name is Maiden Worry. On her travels, all the sorrows of the people are revealed to her. She hears the complaints of the sick, the sighs of the dying, the prayers and curses. Very few people look upon her troubled countenance. It is said that whoever once looks into her eyes can never really be happy again for the rest of their lives.

In those dark days that are being told of now, Maiden Worry had just finished her most difficult tour on the Earth. She heard people speak only bitter and despondent words. Her heart was filled with more and more misery. Her steps became heavier and heavier. Her breathing was ragged. On a path near the Dead Sea, she sank to the earth. As she slowly raised her head again, she gazed with tear-filled eyes upon a blooming patch. She hoped to get some comfort from the beauty of the flowers. A breath of wind carried the voice of Nature toward her. From the flowers, it said, "No human eyes follow a sunbeam into our chalices or give us a friendly look. We wither away unnoticed. The children have forgotten how to weave us into pretty crowns. We are trampled and stomped on the big battlefields. The blood of the people flows down to us like bitter dew."

This was too much for the maiden, that even Nature could no longer give her comfort. Her tears fell to the flowered meadow like sour rain, until finally, in all her despair, she sank into a deep sleep. Then, out of the heavenly heights, God the Father came near to her. He saw what human sorrows filled her virgin heart, and such great sympathy gripped the Heavenly Father that a teardrop slipped from his eye. And He spoke to the sleeping one: "Maiden Worry, take heart! You shall see better times on the Earth. I will send the people my own Son, The Christ, to redeem them." Thus spoke Father God, and disappeared into the clouds.

The teardrop that had fallen from the Divine Eye split into many thousands of droplets. They fell to the depths like glittering rain. The closer they got to Earth, the more lively they became and were transformed. By the time they reached the Earth, they were many thousands of buzzing bees flying over the meadow. The bees immediately visited the flowers, and the flowers happily received these cheerful messengers from Heaven. From the happiness of the flowers sweet nectar welled up and starry perfume spread over the fields of the Earth.

Maiden Worry awoke in the middle of the sweet flower aroma and heard the lovely singing and buzzing of the bees. For the first time since she had been touring the Earth, she smiled, and said, "Sun-happiness has moved in here! Surely it will turn the hearts of mankind again, just as the Divine Father proclaimed."

From then on, the maiden was accompanied by bees on her earthly travels. When bitterness and disappointment overshadowed her soul, they brought her some sun-nectar. Then she would think of the prophecy.

Once, when the darkest night of the year had spread over the Earth, the maiden was wandering over cool fields. All at once she realized that something was illuminating the darkness like a bright light. It was the Light of Bethlehem. Full of wonder, she stood still and looked up at the far-away sky. Crowds of angels were ascending and descending, from Heaven to Earth and back again to the heavenly heights. They carried up the sorrows of the Earth, and brought back a mild light that sank like morning dew into the sleeping people and continued to shine there. And the maiden whispered to herself, "Will the Earth again become a heavenly place?"

She followed the shining beam of the great light and came to a stable where shepherds were just laying their gifts at the foot of a cradle: bread, milk, and a white lamb. She went quietly to a dark corner and listened to the heartfelt words of the shepherds, and her gaze rested upon the Heavenly Child. But, in a single moment, she perceived how a dark, threatening shadow hovered over the peaceful scene. Within the gloomy clouds, the clear form of a cross appeared. And now the maiden understood: "My earthly travels must continue. Darkness is throwing its shadow at the Light. Much affliction will still befall the Earth."

Soon the shepherds said their goodbyes and returned to their flocks. With great care the maiden drew closer to the cradle. The Child gave her a friendly gaze, and His eyes shone in her soul. For her, it was like when the light of spring warms the wintry earth. The maiden left the dingy stable.

From then on, when her path led her through human sorrow and misery, it was not only worry and trouble that filled her heart. She knew that hidden in every person there was a spark of that mild light she had seen raining down from Heaven. She looked for it in light-hearted people as well as the grieving, and she was glad if it grew larger and brighter. You see, she knew that the sparks would one day gather themselves into a great flame, whose light and warmth would dispel all darkness.

That is how the legend is told. Years later, John the Baptist baptized people in the Jordan River. It is said that the first nourishment he gave to Christ after the baptism was honey from wild bees—honey, the most precious gift of the Earth.

DEATH OF A BEEKEEPER
IN LIEU OF AN EPILOGUE

My father introduced me to beekeeping as a boy. I was his fetch and carry boy. When I was about ten years old, he gave me a beehive that I was to care for myself. The hive was lodged in a white box. My older brother had his hive in a blue box next to mine.

A few years later, when I had been at teacher's college in Bern, Switzerland, for only about two weeks, my father died suddenly of a stroke. It was in May, when everything was in bloom. And yet, all twelve of the beehives at our house died with him. Not one bee flew out any more. Sadly, I realized this only after two weeks when I had returned home. Suddenly, I saw that a swarm had flown up and was getting ready to settle into my white box. They were tirelessly carrying out dead bees, as if to say: "We are here again—carry on!"

It is true; out of all the hive boxes, the swarm chose mine. Gradually, I cleaned out all the other hive boxes of dead bees. And so, I also became a beekeeper. Out of that first swarm, seven new hives were formed in the following years.

Later, I heard about an old superstition that says when a beekeeper dies, one should knock three times on each hive and say this verse:

Bee, bee, my father is dead,
Do not leave me in my need!

Bien, Bien, myn Att isch tot,
Verlass mi nid i myner Not!

Because I continued to care for those bees, later on I was able to write the books *Little Bee Sunbeam* and *The Bee Book* so that young people could become familiar with the wondrous life of bees.

— Jakob Streit

Translator's note: The German word *Bienenvater* translated literally means "bee father." In English we use the word "beekeeper."